GOOGLE ADWORDS GOTCHAS:

Five Ways AdWords Wastes Your Money, and How to Avoid Them

A 299 GUIDE

2014 EDITION

by Jason McDonald, Ph.D.
© 2014, JM Internet Group
www.jm-seo.org
510-713-2150

Table of Contents

Prologue

Before we begin...

This is a completely **unofficial** guide to Google AdWords. Google has not endorsed this guide, nor has Google nor anyone affiliated with Google been involved in the production of this guide.

That's a good thing. This guide is **independent**. My aim is to "tell it as I see it," giving you no-nonsense information on the "gotchas" I see lurking of AdWords that may cost you money – a lot of money, if you are not careful!

In addition, please note the following:

- All trademarks are the property of their respective owners. I have no relationship with nor endorsement from the mark holders. Any use of their marks is so I can provide information to you.

- Any reference to or citation of third party products or services whether for Google AdWords, or otherwise, should not be construed as an endorsement of those products or services tools, nor as a warranty as to their effectiveness or compliance with the terms of service of Google AdWords.

The information used in this guide was derived in Spring and Fall, 2013, and Spring, 2014. However, Google AdWords and Google itself changes rapidly, so please be aware that scenarios, facts, and conclusions are subject to change without notice.

Additional Disclaimer. Internet marketing is an art, and not a science. Any changes to your Internet marketing strategy, including SEO, Social Media Marketing, and AdWords, is at your own risk. Neither Jason McDonald nor the JM Internet Group assumes any responsibility for the effect of any changes you may, or may not, make to your website or AdWords advertising based on the information in this guide.

Now that we've covered the background, *let's get started.*

Sobriety

A man walks into a bar... We've all heard *that* series of jokes. Here's one of my favorites:

A Panda walks into a bar. He then proceeds to take a drink, pulls out a gun, and shoots everyone else in the bar. The bartender survives, pops his head up and asks, "Why did you do that?" The panda replies, "Just Google 'Panda'": *large black and white mammal native to China. Eats shoots and leaves."*

Here's another one:

Three men walk into the Googleplex. They've been invited to a "Learn with Google AdWords Seminar," and Google has decided to hold the seminar on the Google campus, complete with hors d'ouevres and a full bar offering expensive beers, wine, and liquor. The three men sit down, order some free drinks, and start venting their frustrations as small businessmen in today's online world.

The first man says, "I inputted my AdWords keyword as "joint repair," and I got clicks for "knee joints," and "hip joints," when what I do is repair *automobile* CV joints." **The bartender chuckles.**

The second man chimes in, "You think that's bad. I set up my ad for my local veterinarian business, and I was running not just on Google but on parked domains, error pages, and animated game sites in China, and I didn't even know it!" **The bartender chuckles.**

The third man looks around a little nervously, and says, "I tried AdWords but then I asked my customers, and they all said that they ignore ads entirely, and click on the organic links, so I hired an SEO company and $25 K later, I can't tell which clicks are from ads and which ones from SEO, if any." **The bartender chuckles.**

Frustrated, the three look at the bartender and say, "What are you laughing at?" The bartender just stands there and smiles. Increasingly frustrated, the three start growling, "**WHAT ARE YOU LAUGHING AT?**"

Finally the bartender says: "I work at Google, I'm here to teach the seminar, and *I get paid no matter what.* Let's get started."

ADWORDS IS LIKE ALCOHOL

AdWords, you see, is like **alcohol**, and **Google** is like the **bartender**. Google is serving up the "drinks" on Google.com as users enter search queries, advertisers bid to show on relevant queries, and Google displays ads in a bidding war of one advertiser against another.

Every time a user clicks on an AdWords ad, Google gets paid.

- *Regardless of whether the click ends in a sale, Google gets paid.*

- *Regardless of whether the click ends in a sales lead, Google gets paid.*

- *Regardless of how it all ends up, Google gets paid.*

Regardless, regardless, regardless: **Google gets paid.** You, the advertiser, in contrast make money if, *and only if*, that click leads towards a sale in some way, shape, or form.

Now wait a second, doesn't Google care about Quality Score, effective advertising, and all that? Doesn't the corporate charter say "don't be evil?" Aren't ads shown only on keywords that you determine as an AdWords advertiser?

Well, yes and no. Like so many things in life, AdWords is a lot more complicated than it seems. Like so many things involving big, powerful corporations, the reality is a lot more complicated than the corporate marketing-speak would have you believe.

Just like in the liquor and entertainment industry, there is a lot more going on than just helpful bartenders helping happy customers get a little buzzed.

Consider this reality: Google gets paid *by the click*, but you get paid by the sale.

Those are not the same thing.

Let's bring it back to a simple analogy: Google is like the bartender. If you were to walk into a bar, and order up a drink, *any drink*, would you expect the bartender to serve up his cheapest or his most expensive drink? If you accidentally gave him a $100 bill, thinking it was just a $10, and said, "Keep the change," would you expect him to run out after you and make sure you meant to give him a $100 and not a $10?

Of course not.

If you are looking to buy a used car, would you rely on the used car salesman to be an objective source of information on used cars?

Of course not.

So when it comes to AdWords why are so many people so trusting that Google has set up everything fair and square?

Don't ask me. I know how to advertise, correctly, on AdWords and make money off of it. But those poor, unfortunate trusting souls who shower Google with unnecessary cash, must just trust Google because of technology, brand image, and all those fun stories of Googlers playing foosball and having fun at the Googleplex. Fun, happy people can't be evil, right?

I don't think Google is evil. Don't get me wrong. But having taught thousands of students online, interacted with many others via YouTube, led workshops and classes in the Bay Area, and engaged many businesses as an AdWords consultant, I have encountered frustrated businessperson after frustrated businessperson (and quite a few frustrated non-profits). People who have been burned by AdWords:

> People who **wasted thousands of dollars** on AdWords advertising without every really understanding how keywords work in AdWords.

> People who were running on **Google's Display Network**, throwing away dollar after dollar, without even knowing it.

> People who poured thousands into AdWords, only to ultimately realize that **SEO (Search Engine Optimization), Facebook, LinkedIn or even Social Media Marketing** worked much better for them.

I have had clients who advertised "adult diapers" (without knowing it, as a medical supply service) when they really made their money on "autoclaves." Clients who ran on "IP" for Intellectual Property and got clicks for "Internet Protocol." And clients who ran on "knee surgery" that got clicks for CV joints for cars, and clicks on game websites from Japan and China focused on virtual surgery.

ARE YOU BEING GOT BY THE ADWORDS GOTCHAS?

If you are advertising on AdWords, you - too - may be running in all sorts of crazy ways, being "got" by the AdWords gotchas, without ever realizing it. AdWords is like alcohol, and like an alcoholic, you might be in a lot more trouble than you realize!

This book will test your knowledge of AdWords via the "AdWords Sobriety Test" to determine if you are sober, tipsy, or totally drunk when it comes to Google AdWords. This book will guide you through the five major gotchas inside of AdWords, each a "trap" into which you can fall and into which you can throw money into an endless, useless pit.

The five **AdWords gotchas** are:

1. (Bad) **Match Types**

2. Running on The **Display Network** (without understanding it)

3. **Enhanced Campaigns** (specifically running on mobile search)

4. **Poorly Written Ads** (that attract but do not repel)

5. **Failure to Consider Alternatives** (namely, failing to measure your AdWords return-on-investment vs. SEO, other advertising alternatives, and social media marketing)

Google has built AdWords in such a way that unless you know where to look, unless you know the geeky hard-to-use AdWords interface, you are very likely (almost certainly likely) to set up your AdWords campaigns in such a way that you generate a lot of frivolous clicks that cost you money (and make Google money) without really helping you .

But **friends don't let friends drive drunk**, and friends don't let friends advertise on AdWords without first understanding the five **AdWords gotchas** that can cost you money.

This book, my friend, is my AdWords intervention, my treatise to help you (and others) waste less money on AdWords and be a better advertiser.

Before we dive in, let's get this straight. **I am not against AdWords.**

AdWords can be great. AdWords can be very cost-effective. Like a fine California wine complementing a fine meal, AdWords can do amazing, wonderful things for your online marketing strategy. Like a powerful martini or unusual cocktail, AdWords can accomplish things that other tactics like SEO or Social Media Marketing just can't get done.

Drink responsibly and you can do amazing things. But drink irresponsibly and incredibly bad things can happen. Note that this book is not, therefore, about the positive with respect to AdWords. It is only about the negative, the five gotchas to avoid at all costs.

Let's get Started!

>> About the Author

>> Acknowledgements

>> Get Free Stuff

>> Copyright and Disclaimer

About the Author

My name is Jason McDonald. I teach courses on SEO (Search Engine Optimization), AdWords, and Social Media Marketing both online and in the San Francisco Bay Area, including a very popular course called "Marketing without Money" at Stanford Continuing Studies. I love teaching and explaining things, having received my Ph.D. from the University of California, Berkeley, in 1992 and my A.B. from Harvard University in 1986. I have worked as a technology journalist since 1994, at a very small start-up focused on embedded systems, all of which increased my passion for all things Internet and for explaining marketing, advertising, and free publicity across search engines, social media sites, and other media. You can find my books on Amazon, my "how to" tutorials on YouTube, and you can reach out to me at JasonMcDonald.org, my corporate site at JM-SEO.org, or just call 510-713-2150.

Acknowledgements

I want to thank Noelle Decambra, my beloved wife, for her assistance in editing the guide and researching the materials as well as Gloria McNabb for her help covering phones and emails for an author too busy to do it all himself. I would also like to thank my students, who by their questions, enthusiasm, and puzzled looks have inspired me to never stop learning. Leonard Rogers of Acorn Studios (Sacramento, California) is responsible for formatting of this ebook. As usual, Len made a complex graphic design task seem easy. Thank you all.

Get FREE Stuff & Take the AdWords Sobriety Test

We produce a lot of free content at the JM Internet Group. Here's how to be alerted of free items as we produce them –

- Sign up for our **free** email alerts at http://jm-seo.org/free. Then, when we release a new 299 Guide, you will receive an email alert of our advance review copies.

- Take our free companion **AdWords MOOC** (Massive Open Online Course) available at http://www.jm-seo.org/free to learn the basics of effective advertising on Google AdWords.

- Take one of our **paid** training classes on SEO, Social Media Marketing, and/or AdWords. Everyone who takes our classes will have **free** access to **all** the guides in the series. (Find out more at http://jm-seo.org).

- Use a **coupon code**, available from someone who:
  (a) is already on our mailing list,
  (b) purchased a copy of this guide, or
  (c) took our classes.

Sobriety Test Time

Take the **AdWords sobriety test**. Is your company *drunk, tipsy,* or *sober* when it comes to AdWords? Take the free AdWords Sobriety test at http://jm-seo.org/4 and find out!

Questions? Email info@jm-seo.org, click http://jm-seo.org/44, or call 510-713-2150. As someone who loves to teach, I work really hard for my students and readers, so I strongly encourage you to email me with any questions. Don't hesitate!

 Copyright and Disclaimer Acknowledgements

AN UNOFFICIAL GUIDE
NOT ENDORSED BY GOOGLE

Keywords

Keywords drive search, just like drink orders drive a bar.

If you order a "vodka collins," you are telling the bartender that you want a drink made out of vodka, sour mix, soda water, perhaps an orange or lime for garnish and a maraschino cherry. You are not asking for a "whiskey sour" which is just whiskey, lemon juice and sugar syrup. And of course you can be more specific, clarifying that you want "Grey Goose Vodka" or "Stolichnaya Vodka." You might even use some slang like "Stoli" rather than "Stolichnaya Vodka," and you might misspell "Gray Goose" (with an "a" rather than the correct "e").

You get the point: you want what you want, and you don't expect the bartender to substitute *whiskey* for *vodka, vodka* for *whiskey*, or *Smirnoff* vodka when you asked for a *Stoli!* You'd be pretty mad if you ordered a "Grey Goose Vodka" and instead he substituted a cheaper brand, or he watered it down with H2O!

As an advertiser, you expect Google to behave like a trustworthy bartender: serving up your ads on exactly the keywords you specify, and certainly not engaging in any hanky panky substitutions.

You'd expect that, but you'd be wrong. *Say it ain't so, Joe. Say it ain't so.*

In this chapter, we'll learn that in AdWords a *keyword* isn't really a *keyword*, at least not in the way that most advertisers think.

Keywords Drive Search

Keywords drive Google search. Customers enter search queries into Google search, advertisers bid against each other based on keywords, and Google charges for clicks based on how users click from Google to your website on the basis of the match between the searcher keyword query and the keyword that you bid on.

Right?

Well not exactly. Let's break this down.

First, there's the **searcher** (consumer), and he might enter into Google something like "knee pain," "knee surgery," or perhaps "best knee surgeons in San Francisco." He is essentially giving an order to Google to go out and find the "best matches" for that query. Google, acting like the bartender, serves up the order, so to speak, by providing both organic and paid results. The organic results, of course, are the non-paid results which occur in the center of the page, and the advertising results via AdWords usually occur at the top and top right of a Google search page.

As the **advertiser**, you are a bit like the drink manufacturer, the Stolichnaya Vodka or the Grey Goose Vodka, that wants your drink to be served. You are certainly going to need a good relationship with the bartender, and you want to have him serve up your drinks instead of those of your competitors!

Inside of AdWords, you tell Google the keywords that interest you by entering them into the AdWords interface via **match types**.

Here's where it gets interesting. You'd think that if you enter keywords into your AdWords account (at the group level) in the following way that you would be giving very clear instructions to Google:

knee surgeon

You'd think that you'd be telling Google to show your ads if, and only if, the searcher enters the words "knee surgeon" in his query, perhaps "best knee surgeon" would also work or "knee surgeons" (plural), or "knee surgeons for sports injuries." But definitely the two words "knee" and "surgeon" would have to be present in the search query. You'd think that, wouldn't you?

But you'd be wrong.

Entering knee surgeon as your AdWords keywords lets Google "think for you" and Google might actually run your ads on keyword queries such as:

knee surgeon
orthopedic surgeon
hip surgeon
hip surgery
leg surgery
leg surgeons
shoulder surgery

Leg surgery isn't exactly a great match for *knee surgeon*, is it? But that is definitely a possibility as are many other search queries that can be very, very far from what you told Google.

Entering keywords into AdWords without understanding match types is a very dangerous strategy! Perhaps you do only surgery on knees, so why does it show your ad for a search such as hip surgery, or leg surgery?

WHEN IS A KEYWORD NOT A KEYWORD?

Why is this so? Why does Google play so loosey-goosey with your keywords?

The answer is that Google makes money off of **clicks**; whereas you make money off of **conversions**. Those are not the same thing.

Google is interested in pushing as many ads as possible across the page, and it takes a very liberal approach with AdWords advertisers who give it free reign: those who just enter keywords into the interface with no [brackets], no "quotes", and no +plus +signs.

Most advertisers haven't a clue about match types in AdWords, and they are giving Google free reign to "think for them."

You might be an orthopedic surgeon who is focused solely on knee surgery... but Google thinks it's just as likely that people might search for *knee, hip, shoulder, orthopedic* in combination with *surgeon, surgery,* and even pain.

You enter knee surgeon *and think those are your AdWords keywords.*

Google takes knee surgeon *and starts doing some pretty crazy substitutions.*

You get a lot of clicks, pay Google a lot of money, but you do not get a lot of sales inquiries for knee surgeons.

If you don't tell Google your precise order... it will run away with you, just as if you walk into a bar and say to the bartender, "give me a drink, any drink," he is likely to serve you up one of his most expensive concoctions.

MATCH TYPES
GIVE PRECISE ORDERS TO GOOGLE

Understanding **match types** is the first part of the AdWords Sobriety Test, and most advertisers fail. They just enter their keywords willy-nilly without thinking through their keywords, and without reigning Google in via very specific keyword instructions.

Let's investigate.

 Match Types Explained

When you enter your keywords into AdWords (which, of course, you do at the campaign > ad group > keyword tab level), you are telling Google which keyword queries you'd like to bid on. Ads are displayed on Google search as a function of three variables: **keywords, bid**, and **quality score** (more on that later).

To see what's going on, log into AdWords, create an Ad Group, or click on an existing group, click over to the keyword tab and enter your keywords. Let's say you own a "cat boarding" establishment in San Francisco, and so you enter keywords such as:

> *cat boarding*
> *board cats*

You think you have indicated to Google to run your ad if, and only if, the searcher enters the words "cat" and "boarding" right? Other words are OK, but at least the words cat and boarding, right?

Wrong.

You've only given an *indication* to Google, a *suggestion* to Google (not a a firm order). Just as if you said to the bartender, you'd like a *Whiskey Collins* but really *just fish me up a drink any old drink*, and you can put *whatever Whiskey you like in there*, fellow.

Would you trust the bartender? Would you trust the bartender drink after drink, day after day, week after week?

If you do not enter [brackets], "quotes," or +plus +signs around your keywords in AdWords, you are saying to Google:

Google AdWords, I have complete trust and faith in you, so please think for me.

But in our cat boarding example, Google might actually run your ad on search queries such as:

> *cat boarding*
> *pet boarding*
> *dog boarding*
> *iguana boarding*
> *cat veterinarians*
> *cat vets*

You might get clicks, but you'll get a lot of bounces from people looking for *dog boarding or iguana boarding,* not to mention *cat veterinarians.*

How do you fix this? By understanding **match types**. Here is an explanation of what each match type tells Google AdWords:

[cat boarding] = run my ad if, and only if, the only two words entered are cat boarding. That's it. Nothing else! (**exact match**)

"cat boarding" = run my ad if, and only if, they enter the phrase "cat boarding" as well as other words before, or after, but not in the middle. (**phrase match**)

+cat +boarding = run my ad if, and only if, they enter the word cat and the word boarding. Google is allowed simple substitutions (called stemming) for cats (plural) or board (vs. boarding), but Google is not allowed to substitute pets for cat, or vet for boarding, etc. (**broad match with modifier**)

-cheap = do not run my ad if they enter the word cheap, regardless of whatever other words they enter. (**negative match**)

And the bad boy:

> **cat boarding** = Google, run my ad for search queries like cat boarding but also think for me, and feel free to make substitutions such as pet for cat, or even perhaps iguana for cat, or vet for boarding. (**broad match**).

What you want to do is to "speak Google," and use [brackets], "quotes," or +plus +signs around your keywords in AdWords to give very specific orders to Google.

But that's not what most people do. They just enter their keywords without anything around them, at all.

BROAD MATCH MEANS YOU REALLY TRUST IN GOOGLE

Here's an example from a real AdWords advertiser experience. An advertiser came to us who wanted to run on negotiation training to reach business executives and corporate types. They had just entered those words, no brackets, quotes, or plus signs into Google AdWords.

Here's a sample of phrases for which Google actually ran their ads and for which they paid for clicks:

> *debt settlement training*
> *union bargaining training*
> *contract negotiation seminar*
> *hostage negotiation training*
> *negotiation mock up class*

Oops! Someone looking for negotiation mock up class isn't exactly an appropriate target for a business negotiation course. *Debt settlement training* isn't exactly appropriate either! What happened is that they didn't understand match types, including negative keyword matches. They got clicks but not that many conversions, and wasted a lot of money.

> **VIDEO.** Watch a quick video tutorial on AdWords Match Types at http://jm-seo.org/2999-w

Many advertisers are burning through **hundreds**, possibly **thousands**, of dollars per month on bad match types. And what's worse: they don't even know it.

They are paying Google for irrelevant clicks, Google is making a lot of money off of this... and the advertisers are simply "in the dark."

It's sad, and it's true. But there is a simple technique you can use to avoid this: **do not ever use the broad match type**. At a minimum, always **add the "+" plus sign in front of each and every keyword** in your AdWords account.

+KEYWORD =
GOOGLE RUN ONLY ON
THAT KEYWORD

Simply adding a "+" sign to your keywords fixes the Google-running-away-with-your-money-problem.

 Finding Your Actual Keyword Matches

But what if you didn't understand match types, and you ran on broad match, can you find out the words or phrases that Google actually has been running your ads on? Yes, you can. You just need to know where to look in AdWords.

If you're like most advertisers, you set up your ad using broad match as your match type. You trusted Google, and you maybe got a little drunk on AdWords seeing all those clicks from Google into your website.

But something just never felt right. Lots of clicks, lots of money spent, but not that many registrations or sales. What could be going wrong?

Bad match types is one possible culprit. You can drill down in AdWords and see the exact search queries users entered into Google. Here's how.

1. Log into AdWords.

2. Click on a **Campaign**, then on an **ad group**.

3. Click on the **keywords tab**.

4. Find the **details tab** in the middle of the page and click on it.

5. Under search terms, click **all**.

Presto! Now you can see the actual search terms Google ran your ad on. You can adjust your time horizon in the top right corner for more than one month if there is insufficient data, and you can select an individual keyword by checking the box next to your keyword prior to step #4 above.

Your matches will be indicated by:

Exact match = they entered those words, and nothing else.
Phrase match = they entered those words as a phrase plus words before or after.
Broad match = Google did some thinking for you, whether good or bad.

Check your own AdWords keyword match types, and decide how badly broad match is damaging the efficiency of your campaign. I recommend broad match only for advanced advertisers who have a strategic reason for it, and who commit to monitoring it on a weekly basis.

 Understanding Negative Match Types

Negative keywords are another important strategy in AdWords, yet most advertisers do not use them. Negative keyword match types are an easy way to get rid of non-customers. If you enter a minus sign in front of a keyword in AdWords you are telling Google to not show your ad if they enter that word. A negative keyword is a stop word, so to speak. So:

–cheap

In our cat boarding example, would mean do not show our ad if they enter keyword phrases such as:

cheap cat boarding
board my cat cheap in San Francisco

Who wants to sell to cheap people? Free is another common negative keyword.

NEGATIVE KEYWORDS
ARE STOP WORDS

Have you identified any negative keywords? Have you designated them in AdWords?

Where do you do so? Again, Google doesn't make this easy. Google hides negative keywords at the very, very bottom of the keywords tab in AdWords. Click on a group, then the keywords tab, and then on the very bottom left you'll see in blue Negative keywords. Click there and you can add negative keywords at either the campaign or group level. If there are words like cheap or free or other helper words that clearly tell you someone is not your customer, be sure to enter these keywords as negatives. You can read Google's help file on negative keywords at http://jm-seo.org/299-a3.

 AdWords Sobriety Quiz:

It's time to take a quiz. Is your company **sober, tipsy,** or **drunk** when it comes to keywords in AdWords?

Match Types. Are you running on broad match, exact match, phrase match, broad match with modifier? If you are running only on broad match, you're drunk. If you are running on other match types (especially phrase match or modified broad match (+)), you're sober.

Negative Match Types. Have you identified negative keywords? Have you entered them into AdWords? If so, you're sober. If not you're tipsy, if not drunk.

Keyword Reporting. Do you run regular reports that indicate the actual search queries users enter, and do you use that data to refine your AdWords campaign? If you do so on a regular basis (e.g., monthly), you're sober. If you have run them once, your tipsy. If never, you're drunk.

Take the sobriety test online at http://jm-seo.org/4 or begin your learning journey with our free AdWords MOOC / Tutorial at http://jm-seo.org/67.

Display Network

Advertising on AdWords is advertising on *Google.com*, right?

Wrong.

Advertising on Google via AdWords can actually place your ads across a range of sites, including:

Google.com, Google.ca, Google.co.in and every other Google for every other country on earth.

AOL.com, Earthlink.net and other Google "search partners."

NYTimes.com, Chicagotribune.com, hotair.com, weather.com, boss-ip.com, gmail.com, and thousands of other websites in the Google "Display Network."

Parked domains, error pages, forums, photo- and video-sharing pages, juvenile, gross and bizarre sites, sexually suggestive sites and other less obvious sites in the "Display Network"

Remarketing by showing your ads to people based on a) their search history on Google.com, b) their search or browse history across the Google Network, and/or c) cookies you have had placed on their browsers via a "remarketing list."

Choice is a good thing, right? Well that depends whether you pro-actively authorized the choice or not, whether the choice turns out to be a good one in terms of return-on-investment, whether you go into the choice open-eyed, understanding what you are doing, and whether there is transparency in terms of results so you can pro-actively make intelligent choices about your advertising dollars.

Meet the **Display Network**, where none of the above usually apply.

THE DISPLAY NETWORK:
GOOGLE'S DIRTY LITTLE SECRET

How can this be so? Well before we dive into what the Display Network is and how it actually works (vs. how Google claims it works), we need to understand how most advertisers turn it on without really knowing that they have done so.

The reason is arguably the most misleading statement in all of AdWords: "Best opportunity to reach the most customers."

You see, when an advertiser sets up a new campaign in AdWords, the default setting is to turn ON the Display Network. Most advertisers simply follow the default setting, and most advertisers mistakenly assume that an ad running on AdWords means an ad running only on Google.com.

But that's not true.

Many advertisers automatically enroll themselves in the Display Network because when they set up an new campaign in Google AdWords, Google prompts them in the little pull-down menu after you click the green box + Campaign, to run on

Search Network with Display Select
Best opportunity to reach new customers

Is it really the "best opportunity to reach new customers?" I think not.

Let's analyze that phrase:

Best opportunity to reach the most customers.

Did Google say, "cheapest opportunity to reach the most customers?" Or did Google say "best ROI in terms of getting sales or sales leads"? Nope. They just said it's the best way to reach the most customers.

BEST OPPORTUNITY
ISN'T THE CHEAPEST OPPORTUNITY

Implicit might be: most expensive way to reach the most customers. Or best way for Google to make the most money off of you, but not necessarily the best way for you to maximize the ROI (return-on-investment) of your advertising dollar.

Remember: what's good for Google isn't necessarily what's good for you.

This default choice in Adwords - running on both Google's Search Network (which is Google itself plus some search sites like AOL) and Google's Display Network (which is a crazy patchwork of blogs, portals, news sites, parked domains, error pages, sexual and violent sites... you get the picture) - well, this default choice isn't the smartest choice for most advertisers!

Yet the tragedy is that many advertisers set up their AdWords campaigns, naively following Google's advice and selecting the "Search and Display" option, without understanding the critical differences between the two and all the dangers that lurk in the Display Network.

Let's investigate.

 ### Search vs. Browse

When a potential customer goes to Google, he or she types a query into Google. She's in **search** mode. Let's say she's looking for a place to board her precious cat, Fluffy, while she leaves San Francisco to go on vacation in Chicago. She might type into the Google search box:

cat boarding

As we have learned in Chapter One, however, you have to set your match type correctly as an AdWords advertiser to +cat +boarding to prevent Google from running wild with your bids and placing your ad on less relevant (or entirely non-relevant) search queries such as:

pet boarding
dog boarding
cat vets
iguana vets

If you do your homework, and set your match types correctly, you are in decent shape on Google.com as well as Google.ca, Google.co.uk and sites like AOL.com and Earthlink.net whose search engine is actually powered by Google. (You can geotarget those in, or out, depending on what you want in AdWords, by the way).

Those sites are what Google calls the Search Network: Google.com, all the Google's across the world (e.g., Google Canada at Google.ca), and sites like AOL.com that run Google search as their search engine.

But, there's another way to reach this potential customer, however, and it's called the **Display Network**.

Unlike the Google Search Network, the Display Network is built around *browse* rather than *search*.

SEARCH (GOOGLE)
VS.
BROWSE (DISPLAY NETWORK)

Browse occurs when a person is in **read** or **browse** mode on non-Google sites. Suppose, for example, that your Susie Searcher pauses her Google search to find Fluffy a good cat boarding place in San Francisco, and she clicks over to *ChicagoTribune.com* to read the latest news about the Windy City. The Chicago Tribune partners with Google and serves ads across its pages. You can find these ads by browsing pages on ChicagoTribune.com, hovering your mouse over ads, and looking for the URL at the bottom left of the screen. You'll see something like:

http://www.googleadservices.com/pagead/aclk?

Or suppose she goes to *Bossip.com, People.com,* or *Dogbreedinfo.com,* or *Rescueme.org,* or even gets a little lost and ends up on *Animalfriends. com,* Toy.com, or Toystuff.com. Suppose she goes to Gmail, YouTube, or has a slightly darker bent and goes to sexually suggestive, violent, or otherwise "adult" content. Your ad can follow her around the Net, and remind her that Fluffy needs a good home while she is off in Chicago.

All of these sites participate in Google's Display Network, and all make sense as an advertising venue for you if, and only if, the following occurs:

1. The potential customer is a **relevant** customer for you (someone who is at some level interested in boarding a cat).

2. She **browses** the site in question.

3. While browsing, she notices your ad, it seems relevant, she **clicks** on it, and lands on your site.

4. She **converts** on your site to a sale or a sales lead.

That's how Google sells the Display Network, and that's how it's supposed to work (and can work), if you know how to set it up properly. But unfortunately most advertisers do not know how to set it up properly, much less that it exists at all, and so their ads "run wild" across the Display Network causing inappropriate clicks and costing them a lot of money.

The Display Network, in short, is even worse than bad match types as a Google gotcha: it will burn through money faster than a forest fire in Yosemite National Park on a hot summer day.

 Dumpster Diving on the Display Network

Most advertisers follow Google's misleading advice and set their campaigns to run both on the Search Network and on the Display Network. What that does is allow Google to go "dumpster diving" for matches to your ads, and it can come back with some really terrible matches.

There are some great values in dumpster diving, but there is a lot of yucky stuff and a lot of dangerous stuff like sharp objects. I think of the Display Network as the **dumpster diving network** on Google: use at your own risk, and wear gloves.

How so?

Even without running a real ad on Google, for instance, you can take a peek into placements (websites) on which Google will want to place your ad across the network.

Login to your Google AdWords account. Click on Tools and Analysis, and then scroll down to *Display Planner*. Enter a keyword phrase (such as *cat boarding*) and hit the blue button *Get ad group ideas*. Click on the tab *Individual targeting ideas*, and you'll see your first indication that something is amiss. For the keyword *cat boarding,* Google gave us these match suggestions:

dog and cat boarding kennel
cheap cat boarding
cat dog pet toy
heated pet cat
dog sitting on cat

Google is a machine, and it's seeing that words like "dog," "cat", and "pet" frequently go together. So it might place your *cat boarding* ad on a site for dogs, or even as site for *pet games or pet supplies.* That's not so bad, until you realize that sites in this network run in the thousands upon thousands of impressions, and if you write a bad ad, you might still get a lot of clicks from confused or curious individuals who have little interest in actually boarding a cat at your cat boarding establishment.

Their mental process might go like this:

Hm, I'm reading about funny graphics of dogs sitting on cats. Oh, look at the interesting ad for cat boarding in San Francisco. Do people really board cats? I'll click over there, yes they do, well I don't actually own a cat, so let me go back to viewing those amusing GIFS of dogs sitting on cats.

Click occurred. Charge to your AdWords account made. Google made money, but you did not.

The Display Network can often mean: bad placements, lots of click, Google makes money, you do not.

It gets worse.

Click on the Placements tab, and you'll see a long row of possible placements. For example:

http://www.vetinfo.com
http://www.puppyfind.com
http://www.nextdaypets.com
http://www.freekibblekat.com
http://www.equinenow.com

I'm not kidding. These are actual sites suggested by Google for the keyword phrase *cat boarding.* Click on some of these such as *equinenow. com* or *freekibblekat.com,* and you'll see that the matched placements can be truly terrible. Equinenow.com is a horse site, which is pretty far afield from cat boarding.

It gets worse.

What Google doesn't show you is that your ad can also start running on many scam sites such as Parked Domains, Error Pages and all sorts of nefarious sites that people build in the Google AdSense network for the sole purpose of attracting advertising dollars and clicks, with little care as to whether these clicks turn into sales or sales leads. In fact, Google has an entire program called AdSense that encourages people to build high traffic sites to serve ads.

THE DISPLAY NETWORK IS DANGEROUS

You can peek behind the curtain and see how aggressively Google markets this concept on the official AdSense channel at http://www.youtube.com/user/InsideAdSense. What's you'll see is a lot of emphasis on placing Google ad units everywhere, and very little emphasis on generating a high return-on-investment for the advertisers as measured by conversions. Ad Sense and the Display Network are all about generating clicks and generating revenue for Google and its partners, with little thought to whether these ads pay off for you, the advertiser.

For examples of Parked Domains, just go to http://www.animal-friends.com or http://www.findmeacat.com. Then check out the official AdWords help file on parked domains, specifically:

> AdWords policy does not allow ads to link to parked domain sites that *display only advertising listings and links, and that don't provide the user with unique and valuable content on the landing page domain.* (Browsed October 20, 2013, http://http://bit.ly/1cLFclr, emphasis added).

Surf back over to http://www.animalfriends.com/ and ask yourself if that site seems to be accordance with Google's policy. There seems to be a lot of "don't ask, don't tell" going on the Google Display Network!

Google is judge, juror, and executioner across the network with a vested interest in high click volume, and few incentives to weed out sites that generate a lot of click volume no matter the method. Enron, meet Google. Google, meet Enron.

My advice: **do not run on the Display Network** unless you are an expert in Google Adwords.

Display Network Gotchas

The Display Network is a big Google gotcha. You sign up for AdWords, set up your campaigns, and mistakenly trust Google and click to be on both Google Search and the Display Network. Here's a summation of the two problem areas:

Badly matched placements. You enter your keywords and Google places you on badly matched, but honest, websites.

Nefarious placements. Google places you on Parked Domains, Error pages, and sites specifically designed to run high volume clicks, possibly even with clickbots and click fraud.

We can't say much for certain about click fraud and fraudulent sites on the Display Network because Google seems to have little interest in transparency about how the Display Network actually operates. You can read their official propaganda at http://www.google.com/ads/displaynetwork/ and at http://jm-seo.org/299-a4.

Inside the Display Planner, type your website address into the box called *Your landing page* and hit *Get ideas*. Sort placements by impressions by week, and you'll often see "Anonymous" as the top recommended site. That tells you something, doesn't it?

Display Network Reporting

Let's say that you are running on the Display Network without having really understood it. (This is commonly true for most novice advertisers). Fortunately, you can run a report and see the actual placements where Google ran your ads. Here's how to do it:

1. Click on the **campaign** you want to investigate.

2. Click on the **Display Network tab** on the far right.

3. Click on the **Placements** tab.

4. Scroll down the list, which you can sort in descending order by clicks, and **copy / paste the URL's** listed into another browser window.

5. Decide if this is a **good** or **bad** placement.

6. If it's a bad placement, click the green dot next to it in AdWords. Change status to excluded (**red ball**).

I call this *weeding the garden*. For an advanced advertiser who does want to reach people in "browse mode," there are values to be had on the Display Network, just like there is a lot of good stuff in the garbage dumpsters of New York City. For most advertisers, however, the trouble of all the bad matches and nefarious sites far outweighs the benefits, especially when compared with cleaner networks such as Facebook or LinkedIn for reaching people when they are in "browse mode."

Managing the Display Network

The Display Network, in short, is not recommended for any but the most skilled advertisers. For most advertisers, I strongly recommend simply deactivating it. To do so:

1. Login to your AdWords account.

2. Select a campaign on the left column.

3. Click on the settings tab.

4. Under Type, use the pull-down menu to change the type to Search Network Only.

Remember to set accurate match types for the search network using brackets, quotation marks, or the plus (+) sign!

If you decide that reaching people in browse mode makes sense, and you do pro-actively want to run on the Display Network, I recommend splitting your campaigns into those on the Google Search Network and other parallel campaigns on the Display Network (for better reporting and keyword management). Then on your Display Network campaign, turn off the nefarious sites as follows:

1.   Login to your AdWords account.

2.   Select a campaign on the left column.

3.   Click on the Display Network tab.

4.   Click on the Placements tab.

5.   Scroll down to the very bottom of the page, and select Campaign Exclusions, Site Category options. Exclude the bad sites such as Parked Domains, Error pages and what not.

Next, after you run on the Display Network for a specific time period, log back into, click over to the Placements tab, and browse your placements for "bad placements." Then turn off these placements by selecting the green ball, and turning it off / red. Over time you can "train" Google to place your ads on the best placements; in my experience, mail.google.com (Gmail), and YouTube.com tend to be the best placements by far.

VIDEO. Watch a quick video tutorial on the Display Network at http:// jm-seo.org/299-a5

 AdWords Sobriety Quiz: Display Network

It's time to take the next quiz. Is your company **sober, tipsy**, or **drunk** when it comes to the Display Network?

Running Blind. Are you running on the Display Network without having any idea what it is? (Remember, you can determine if you are running on the Display Network on the *Campaign Level > Settings > Search & Display Network*). If so, you are definitely drunk.

Deactivated Nefarious Sites. If you are consciously running on the Display Network, have you de-activated parked domains and other nefarious sites? If not, you are tipsy. If so, you are sober.

Display Network Reporting. Do you run regular reports that show your actual placements, and do you "weed the garden" of bad placements? If you do so on a regular basis (e.g., monthly), you're *sober*. If you have run them once, your *tipsy*. If never, you're *drunk*.

Take the sobriety test online at http://jm-seo.org/4 or begin your learning journey with our free AdWords MOOC / Tutorial at http:// jm-seo.org/67.

Enhanced Campaigns

What could possibly be bad about something called *enhanced campaigns*? Well, remember back to High School English when you were required to read George Orwell's novel *1984*?

OK, you weren't paying attention. I get that.

But you should have paid attention in English class. In *1984*, Orwell had a concept called *Doublespeak*, which according to Wikipedia, is "language that deliberately disguises, distorts, or reverses the meanings of words" (http://en.wikipedia.org/wiki/Doublespeak, browsed 28 October 2013). In Orwell's novel, *doublespeak* referred to politicians twisting good-for-them into good-for-you:

War is peace. Peace is war. *Doubleplus good and all that sort of thing.*

Enhanced campaigns were introduced by Google in the summer of 2013, and in many instances *enhanced campaigns* were an unfortunate example of Google using *doublespeak: enhanced* for Google, to generate Google a lot more money, but not necessarily enhanced for advertisers.

Good-for-Google positioned as **good-for-you.**

Enhanced campaigns, in short, are a kind of Google *doublespeak*: not necessarily good for you, despite what Google says.

If you were paying attention in the Summer of 2013, Google asked you to engage in some nifty clicks to "self-upgrade." If not, it automatically upgraded you, whether you liked it or not.

Upgrade to *enhanced campaigns*. More doublespeak: for many advertisers, it was really a *downgrade to enhanced campaigns*.

An *upgrade* that was really a *downgrade; enhanced campaigns* that really took out many useful features (especially device targeting).

What happened? Let's investigate.

Enhanced Campaigns: More Clicks from Mobile Ad-Words

The main impact of *enhanced campaigns* was to "upgrade" every advertisers so that their ads now show on mobile devices by default. Previously, unless you pro-actively chose to advertise on mobile, you were not automatically signed up for mobile devices. Mobile devices refers to not only cell phones but also tablets like Apple's iPad.

With the "upgrade" to enhanced campaigns, the default setting is now to run everywhere: on the desktop, on mobile phones, and on tablets.

But what if?

What if... your website looks terrible on a mobile phone?

What if... your customers aren't using mobile?

What if... your customers might search on mobile, but the process to purchase your product or service is just too complex, so they are likely to abandon or bounce?

What if... your customers are largely on the desktop (PC or Mac) but not on tablets? Or vice-versa?

ENHANCED CAMPAIGNS
=
ENHANCED
PROFITABILITY FOR GOOGLE

The Default to Enhanced Campaigns

When you first set up a campaign in AdWords, the new default setting is to run you on mobile devices *whether you like it or not*. If, for whatever reason, cell phones are not your target, you are forced to run on cell phones and can only switch this off at a later point in the process.

The steps are:

1.   **Login** to your AdWords account.

2.   Click on the +**Campaign** green box to create a new campaign.

3.   Select ***Search Network*** only.

4.   You'll see under *Devices*, the phrase "**Ads will show on all type of devices by default.**"

There is no option to turn your campaign off at this point. Google is not going to make this easy!

Next, set up your campaign. Then once it exists, go back to your campaign as follows and deprecate (reduce) your mobile spend as follows:

1.   Click on the **Campaign Name** on the left-hand column.

2.   Click on the ***Settings*** tab across the middle of the page.

3.   Scroll down to Devices, and click on ***Change mobile bid adjustment***.

4.   In the box that says Mobile devices with full browsers, click into the box in the ***Bid adj***. column. Select ***Decrease*** by and enter 100%.

That, my dear friend, is the Orwellianly easy step to turn off your ads for mobile phones. You are obligated in enhanced campaigns to run on both desktops and on tablets, whether you like it or not.

Device targeting - the ability to choose desktop vs. tablets vs. mobile phones - was abandoned with the "upgrade" to enhanced campaigns. No real explanation for why was forthcoming from Google.

A cynic would say forcing advertisers to run across all platforms was a nice way to boost clicks, and Google earnings. But that's what a cynic would say.

What if you want to run primarily on mobile phones but not on desktop / tablets? You can sort of kludge that. Rather than *decreasing* your bid on mobile phones by 100% you can increase it by up to 300%. So you bid low for desktop / tablet clicks and then AdWords will up your bid by 300% on mobile.

It is not possible to run solely on mobile devices, sadly.

Did I mention that the *enhanced* part of *enhanced campaigns* was a pretty Orwellian trick by Google?

Minor Gotchas in Enhanced Campaigns

To be fair to Google, however, there actually are some *enhanced* features in *enhanced campaigns.*

Enhanced campaigns do have some nice features, such as the ability to "up" your AdWords bids for people geographically near to your business, on a mobile phone, or during certain times of day.

A less important but still costly change has to do with phone numbers. Prior to enhanced campaigns, you could include your phone number in your ad and have ad text that might say something like "Call for special deal." The idea was that if they called, you did not pay for the click, and so you got a free ad click from Google.

CALL EXTENSIONS MEAN GETTING CALLS WITHOUT PAYING GOOGLE

Google did not like that.

So simultaneous with the rollout of Enhanced Campaigns, Google expressly forbade including telephone numbers in AdWords ads. Instead, you were supposed to use a "Call Extension."

To set an extension, click on the **Ad extensions** tab inside of your campaign. In the **View:** tab, select **Call Extensions**. Next as you are editing or entering your call extension data you will see two options to the right of **Show my ad with**:

- *A Google forwarding phone number and use call reporting.*

- *My own phone number (don't use call reporting)*

If you select the first option, any calls will be **charged** like clicks. If you select the second option and someone calls on a desktop, then there is **no charge**. On a mobile phone, it will become a "click to call" link and if they click (guess what), you pay.

In sum, enhanced campaigns made it significantly harder (but not impossible) to incent people to *call* rather than to *click*. And Google wrote the above text in a rather confusing way, without clearly marking that by using a Google forwarding number you will pay dearly for those calls (vs. getting them for free to your own number).

Orwell, meet Google. Google, meet Orwell.

VIDEO. Watch a quick video tutorial on Enhanced Campaigns at http://jm-seo.org/299-a6

 AdWords Sobriety Quiz: Enhanced Campaigns

It's time to take the next quiz. Is your company **sober**, **tipsy**, or **drunk** when it comes to enhanced campaigns?

Running Blind. Is mobile for you? Does your site look good on mobile? And/or are your target customers really using mobile search. If you have tested on this, you are sober. If you have not tested it, you are *drunk*. If you've at least thought about mobile vs. desktop, you are just *tipsy*.

Deactivating Mobile Search. If mobile search is not for you, have you deprecated it by 100%? If so, you are *sober*. If not, you are *drunk*. If you are not sure, you are *tipsy*.

Click to Call. Do you understand the difference between a Google forwarding number (which costs you money for each call) vs. your own phone number? Have you pro-actively made the best choice for you? If so, you are *sober*. If not, you are *tipsy*.

There are many positive strategies regarding enhanced campaigns such as sitelinks or social extensions. Take the sobriety test online at http://jm-seo.org/4 or begin your learning journey with our free AdWords MOOC / Tutorial at http://jm-seo.org/67.

Ad Copy

Remember: Google gets paid by the click, but you get paid by the *conversion (a sale or a sales lead)*. **Clicks and conversions are not the same thing!**

If you walk into a bar, the bartender gets paid by *how much you drink*. He really isn't paid to worry about whether you are *drinking too much*, your drinks are *too expensive for your budget*, or even if the drinks you are ordering *taste good*.

Nope, the bartender makes his money by selling you drinks. Plain & simple.

 Clicks are not Conversions

The bar scenario has its AdWords parallel: Google gets paid by the *click*, whereas you make money by the *conversion* (sale or sales lead). Google worries about whether your ads are making it money, not whether they are making you money. Plain & simple.

To succeed at AdWords without losing your shirt, you have to understand the difference between a click and a *conversion* in a very profound way.

CLICKS MAKE GOOGLE MONEY; CONVERSIONS MAKE YOU MONEY

A *click* is just that: a click *from* Google to your website via an AdWords ad. A *conversion*, in contrast, occurs if, and only if, the person takes the next step. He either a) buys your product, or b) registers and thereby becomes a sales lead. A click is not a conversion, and your CTR (click thru rate, about which Google makes a big deal) is not the same as your **conversion** rate (about which Google makes significantly less noise).

Your **CTR** (click thru rate) measures how many clicks you receive over how many times your ad was shown on Google (impressions), expressed as a percentage. The higher the CTR, the more attractive your ad was to get clicks.

Your **conversion rate**, in contrast, measures how many people *converted* (bought or registered) over how many people landed on your landing page, expressed as a percentage.

Unfortunately, Google tilts the entire AdWords propaganda machine to entice you to worry about your **clicks**, much more so than your **conversions**, when really you should worry much more about conversions than about clicks.

Let's get specific: let's return to our example of a cat boarding company in San Francisco. As an AdWords advertiser, you want to advertise your cat boarding service:

- *Only to people in San Francisco;*

- *Only to cat people (not dog or iguana people);*

- *Only to people interested in boarding their cat;*

- *and only to people with the money to do so (not cheap or poor people).*

Let's assume you turn to AdWords, and let's assume you don't really understand all the gotchas lurking beneath the surface. Let's assume you run on bad match types (e.g., not only *cat boarding* but also *pet boarding, iguana boarding* and everything in between). And let's further assume that you write your ad in such a way that it does not clearly explain you board only cats, for example:

Amazing Pet Boarding
www.http://fluffyboarding.com/FreeNight
Fun for Fluffy, Cheap for You.
San Francisco's Best Pet Boarder.

An ad like that - running on the "wrong" keywords - and written in an ambiguous yet exciting way (*Fun for fluffy, cheap for you*), will do what?

Generate lots of **clicks** for Google (a high CTR).

Generate few **conversions** for you (a lower conversion rate), as the ad gets clicked on by *dog people, iguana people*, and *cheap cat people* all of whom fail to convert.

What's the result? Google makes lots of money off of the clicks (and it's happy), but you are not so happy. Why?

Because Google gets paid by the click, while you get paid by the conversion.

When you contemplate the difference between a click and a conversion, you realize that there is a profound **conflict of interest** between Google and its advertisers: Google wants clicks, while advertisers want conversions.

As we have seen so far, your first lines of defense are:

1.   Focus on late stage "buy" keywords vs. early stage "educational" keywords ("cat boarding" vs. "cats" or "cat toys").

2.   Understand AdWords match types, and set them correctly (+modified +broad).

3.   Do not run on the Display Network.

Furthermore, to improve your ad performance you need to write great ads, using what we call an **Attract/Repel** strategy. But before we turn to that, let's investigate the Quality Score Paradox.

 The Quality Score Paradox Clicks

AdWords help makes a big deal out of "Quality Score," which is supposedly a measurement of ad *quality*. Advertisers get very upset when their Quality Score is low on their ads, measuring just 4, 5 or less on AdWords' ten point Quality Score scale. The scale itself and rating are designed to make advertisers worry about low Quality Scores.

To view the quality score of your ads, select an Ad Group, click on the keywords tab, then click the columns drop-down menu in the center toolbar. Next, select customize columns, attributes, and click add next to Qual. score. Click save. You'll then see a new column showing your Quality Score on a ten point scale.

But what does Quality Score actually mean to Google: an ad that gets more clicks, or an ad that gets more *conversions*?

Take a moment and read the official Google article on Quality Score go to http://www.jm-seo.org/299-a7. Here's the bottom line, quoted from that article:

> In a nutshell, higher Quality Scores typically lead to lower costs and better ad positions. The AdWords system works best for everybody – advertisers, customers, publishers, and Google – when the ads we show are relevant, closely matching what customers are looking for. Relevant ads tend to earn more clicks, appear in a higher position, and bring you the most success (retrieved 1/4/2014).

Sounds nice, doesn't it? Relevant ads, a system that is working best for everyone.

But there is more than meets the eye to Quality Score. If you read the official help article closely, you'll see that the very first item on Google's list of "how we calculate Quality Score" is the keyword's "expected click thru rate" (CTR) and item #2 is the "display URL's past CTR".

Quality Score, you see, as calculated by Google does not measure relevancy. It measures clicks and CTR. Not a word about conversions, nor a word about bounce backs from customers. The chummy summary misrepresents what's really going on: a system that rewards clicks to the detriment of conversions.

QUALITY SCORE:
IT'S ALL ABOUT THE CLICKS

Quality Score isn't really about relevancy: it's about **clicks** and **CTR**, and not really about conversions.

The tension between clicks and conversions, between Google and its advertisers, creates the **Quality Score paradox**: an ad that "repels" non-quality searchers and attracts only "qualified" searchers will underperform an ad that attracts everyone. Therefore, such an ad will have a **lower** Quality Score yet a **higher** conversion rate!

What should you do? How should you work on improving not your Quality Score but your conversion rate?

Besides focusing on keywords correctly and avoiding the Display Network, you need to focus on that very first interaction with the customer: the ad text itself. And that ad text needs to attempt to **attract** relevant customers yet **repel** non-relevant customers, Quality Score be damned.

It is to the **Attract / Repel** strategy that we now turn.

 Attract/Repel Writing Great Ad Copy

What does **writing great ad copy** mean? Google says it's all about relevant ads and getting clicks. Google measures great ad copy by Quality Score, meaning an ad that gets many clicks must be a great ad.

That's true (as far as it goes), but writing great ad copy is also about **attract / repel**. Great ads *attract* quality buyers yet *repel* non-quality clicks. They generate high conversions and high ROI, by running on "late stage" or "transactional" keywords and doing their utmost to attract buyers and not tire-kickers.

Let's return to our example of a San Francisco cat boarding establishment. We want to **attract** clicks from people who

- live in San Francisco (set by geotargeting our ad).

- have cats (not dogs or iguanas), and cats that need to be boarded (set by proper keywords)

- are not cheap, that is customers who are willing to spend the money on a quality cat-boarding experience for their beloved feline (set by Attract / Repel).

We want to **repel** clicks from:

- *non-cat people (e.g., dog people).*

- *cheap people (people who will not spend the money)*

If we were to just focus on Quality Score and clicks, we might write an ad that looked like:

Amazing Pet Boarding
www.http://fluffyboarding.com/FreeNight
Fun for Fluffy, Cheap for You.
San Francisco's Best Pet Boarder.

Google would consider this a great ad: it would get a lot of clicks, and be rewarded with a high quality score due to a high CTR including clicks from dog people and/or cheap people. But that's what Google wants, not what we want.

A better ad would **attract** cat people and **repel** dog people and/or cheap people, for example:

Side Adwords Preview

Quality Cat Boarding
San Francisco's No Dog Allowed.
Not the cheapest, but top-rated.

Central Adwords Preview

Quality Cat Boarding
San Francisco's No Dog Allowed.
Not the cheapest, but top-rated.

By getting the phrases "Cat Boarding" in the ad title plus "no dog allowed" we attract cat people but repel dog people. By indicating we are not cheap, we repel cheap people.

Attract / repel is a critical strategy to effective AdWords advertising. Just remember that strategy will result in a *lower* Quality Score as Google will "penalize you" for the lower click thru rate, but (by now) you don't believe everything Google tells you, so that's OK.

VIDEO. Watch a quick video tutorial on writing great ad copy at
http://jm-seo.org/299-a8

AdWords Sobriety Quiz: Ad Copy

It's time to take the quiz on ad copy. Is your company **sober, tipsy,** or
drunk?

Clicks and conversions. Do you understand the difference
between a *click* and a **conversion**? Can you identify a scenario in
which an ad might get many clicks but few conversions? If so, you are
sober. If not, you are at least *tipsy*.

Quality Score. Google bases Quality Score on long-term click thru
rate (CTR). Explain the Quality Score paradox of how an ad with
a low Quality Score might outperform an ad with a higher Quality
Score. If you can do this, you are *sober*. If not, please stop drinking.

Attract / Repel. Suppose you are a personal injury attorney special-
izing only in medical malpractice. Identify clients you would want to
click on your ads vs. those you would not, and write three AdWords
ad headlines that **attract** the "right kind" of client yet **repel** the
"wrong kind." If you can write these kinds of ads, you are sober.

Writing great ad copy is an essential tool in becoming an effective
advertiser on Google. Take the sobriety test online at http://jm-seo.org/4
or begin your learning journey with our free AdWords MOOC / Tutorial
at http://jm-seo.org/67.

Beyond AdWords

They say that if all you have is a *hammer*, everything looks like a *nail*. So I suppose if you are a *bartender*, then really pretty much the solution to everything is to have a *drink*. Or if you run a system like *AdWords*, pretty much the solution to any marketing problem is to *advertise* on AdWords.

Advertising on AdWords (both Search and Display and now on YouTube) is pretty much Google's answer to everything. That's not surprising: Ford dealerships push Fords, Chevy dealerships push Chevys, and Google pushes AdWords.

FORD DEALERS PUSH FORDS; ADWORDS REPS PUSH ADWORDS

No surprises there.

But who speaks for media that might make you a lot of money but is not necessarily advertising on Google, Facebook, or LinkedIn? In the pre-Internet days, we called this the schism between **advertising** and **public relations**; advertising being how you **paid** your way onto the pages of the New York Times and public relations being how you **earned** your way.

Today, if AdWords is paid advertising, its PR twin is SEO: Search Engine Optimization. If advertising on Facebook or LinkedIn is advertising, the PR twin there is social media marketing.

And if your objective is to achieve the highest ROI, then you've got to consider all alternatives and take what's told to you, skeptically, just as if you were shopping for a car you wouldn't expect the Ford salesman to sell you a Chevy.

Don't expect AdWords to tell you about SEO, nor certainly sell you about SEO and its benefits!

Inventory Your Discovery Paths

How do customers find you? Do they search via search engines like Google or Bing? Or do they ask their friends for recommendations on Facebook, or browse reviews on Yelp or even Amazon? Perhaps they aren't looking for what you have to sell at all - perhaps you have to interrupt them via an annoying TV ad, or even (gasp!) email spam.

Before you settle on AdWords as your preferred scenario, consider the "discovery paths" by which potential customers might find you. Namely:

- **The Search Path** – they actively search for you on search engines like Google or Bing.

- **The Browse Path** – they aren't actively searching for you, but are reading (or viewing) related information, as for example reading about cats on a cat blog, or watching videos on YouTube about how to care for cats (or whatever you're selling).

- **The Recommend Path** – they ask for, and rely heavily upon, the recommendations of friends and family or reviews by strangers on sites like Yelp or Google+ Local.

- **The Share Path** – they love your product or service so much, they pro-actively share it with others especially on social media like Facebook or Twitter.

- **The Interrupt Path** – your product or service is so new, so novel, that they aren't looking for it, do not know enough about it to share... and so your marketing must "interrupt" them via annoying ads on television, radio, or even unsolicited email (spam).

For most businesses, customers find you via not just one but many paths. Let's return to our cat boarding establishment example in San Francisco. We definitely get customers via the "Search Path," meaning when they are planning a trip they go to Google and pro-actively search for *cat boarding San Francisco*. But there is also the recommend path (*Hey Facebook friends... do you know any reputable cat boarders in SF?*), the browse path (*just reading the Chicago Tribune and I saw an ad for your cat boarding establishment, so I clicked*), and even perhaps the share path (*Here's a picture of Fluffy, happy to see me as I returned to pick her up at the cat boarders*).

HOW DO CUSTOMERS
FIND YOU?

Before you settle on AdWords, I recommend sketching out the possible discovery paths, doing some research, and attempting to prioritize which paths are most important for your business. If search or browse matter, then AdWords could be a good marketing vehicle. But if not, not.

And certainly don't expect Google or the "helpful" rep's at AdWords to point you to all available discovery paths. Like a good Ford salesman, they'll sell you a Ford.

 AdWords vs. SEO

Since this is an eBook about AdWords, we'll focus primarily on the search or browse paths, which are the two most relevant to AdWords. (Social Media marketing, in contrast, is excellent at influencing the recommend and share paths, and tactics such as email marketing work best for interruption marketing).

Now here's the rub. Or several rubs about AdWords and SEO.

First, Google makes 95% or more of its revenue from advertising, so it stands to reason that AdWords will garner an enormous marketing budget at Google and get the lion's share of the company's attention (Source: http://investor.google.com/financial/tables.html). SEO, in contrast, makes the company no money and in fact diverts money from paid advertising to a non-revenue activity. Google makes its money off of AdWords, and so you have to consider every public statement by the company, every "helpful" help article as designed to push you towards considering AdWords.

Follow the money, follow the money.

As a result, Google does little to promote SEO ("Search Engine Optimization") which is the art and science of getting your company, product or service at the top of Google's organic results. Admittedly, there is Google Webmaster Tools and there is Matt Cutts, but you have to know to look for these resources and even when you find them, the general message is that SEO is hard, and one shouldn't overly invest in trying to "manipulate" Google.

So the first rub is that SEO is deemphasized by Google, and in practical terms, Google's official propaganda is designed to make you believe that SEO is so difficult that you'd be better of just giving up and... *advertising on AdWords*.

Follow the money and Google's official position on SEO is pretty easy to understand: SEO is so hard, you'd be better off just advertising.

SEO IS THE
FREE STUFF

Secondly, assuming you pursue SEO and actually succeed at positioning your company, product or service in the top organic positions, you'll learn one of Google's dirty little secrets: SEO is much, much more effective on average than AdWords.

Most of the time, any company garnering any of the top three positions in organic results for a Google search, will far, far outperform the AdWords ads on the same page. Being in the top three is like winning the Google Olympics; making it to page one is also incredibly helpful. Years ago, AOL (which uses Google as its search engine) leaked a report that indicated that the top three organic positions garnered around 67% of the search traffic; the fact that, to date, Google has never released detailed, realistic data about click behavior (organic vs. paid), is proof positive that organic results generally outperform AdWords.

Or, just ask your friends, family, colleagues: when you do a Google search do you tend to click on the ads or on the organic results? It will be a rare friend who says that he looks at the ads and clicks on the ads. The reality is that organic, SEO results generally outperform AdWords.

Third, in my own experience and in that of my clients, getting a company to the top of Google - while not easy, is not rocket science - and once accomplished, if you measure the return-on-investment of dollars / effort spent vs. conversions achieved, it is no contest: SEO far, far outperforms AdWords - in quantity, in quality, and in return-on-investment.

So if you can succeed at SEO, by all means do so.

That said, are there situations that still merit AdWords? Of course there are. Here are a few:

- **Short tail keywords** like "mortgage rates" vs. long tail keywords like "Credit Unions that offer mortgages in Tulsa, Oklahoma). It is often the case that when combined with geotargeting, advertising on short tail keywords may be the only way to get in front of customers for these short tails.

- **Geotargeting.** AdWords can be a wonderful way to target your message to people in a specific city or state.

- **Speed to the Top.** AdWords can get you to the top of Google in a few hours, while SEO can take weeks or months of sustained effort.

- **Buy or Shopping Keywords.** Some types of keywords (such as "Digital Cameras") tend to provoke user behavior of actually viewing ads over organic results.

These are just a few, but the general point still stands: SEO, in general, outperforms AdWords ads in terms of clicks and in terms of ROI. That doesn't make it easy, but it does earn it a seat at your marketing table as you plan budget and time expenditures.

Just don't expect Google to tout the advantages of SEO! Just remember that SEO has no marketing budget of its own vs. the colossal marketing budget of AdWords.

 AdWords and Other Discovery Paths

Beyond the search path, how does AdWords compare to other paths of discovery? Take, for example, the **browse** path. Users really do read the *Chicago Tribune* or *People* magazine online, and Google can get your ad onto those sites via the Display Network. Therefore, with the caveat that the Display Network should be used with caution, it is true that AdWords can get you in front of people as they browse. This is something not easily achieved through public relations or SEO.

But take the gigantic growth of social media. If people are searching for a pizza restaurant, they might just type "Pizza" into Google, or "Pizza" into Yelp. In that situation **reviews** matter immensely (companies with more reviews and better reviews get the business), and AdWords is not capable of helping you with reviews and your social media / SEO position. Similarly, people often **share** tips, tricks, and preferences via social media like Facebook or LinkedIn, and again in those situations, people are as wary of ads as they are trusting of recommendations from close friends or associates. AdWords does little on social media platforms (with the exception of YouTube), and so if social media really matters to your company, social media marketing (the "free stuff") or advertising on Facebook, LinkedIn, or Twitter (the "paid stuff") might be a better choice than AdWords.

The point here is not that AdWords, with all its faults, is a waste of money or time. It's that smart marketers will consider every possible marketing avenue - free vs. paid, search vs. social - before creating a marketing mix that covers all bases. AdWords might be a small part of a successful marketing plan; just remember it has an enormous marketing budget of its own. No one speaks for free SEO, nor for free social media, certainly not with the zillions of dollars that back up paid advertising on Google, Facebook, Twitter, or LinkedIn.

So tune out (or in) the message accordingly!

 ## Metrics, Metrics, Metrics

Good marketers measure. How do people find your website? What makes them convert? Do more people come from free efforts like SEO or social media marketing, or from paid efforts like AdWords advertising or advertising on Facebook? Which converts more people, and why? To Google's credit, the company provides an amazing, free metrics platform, Google Analytics (http://www.google.com/analytics). When used appropriately, Analytics can answer these questions.

Generally, you'll find that the free efforts outperform the paid ones in terms of ROI, but of course that depends on your specific situation. Regardless, however, don't take anyone's word for what works: not mine, not Google AdWords, not your Yelp sales rep. Set up a marketing plan - free, paid, Google, Bing, Yelp, Facebook - and measure what works. Put your blood, sweat, and tears into what works and base that effort not on hunches but on real facts.

The final gotcha on AdWords is naiveté: taking Google's words that AdWords is your best marketing method, when it might be SEO or Social Media.

 AdWord Sobriety Quiz: Beyond AdWords

It's time to take the final quiz. Is your company **sober, tipsy**, or **drunk** when it comes to considering alternatives and measuring results?

Discovery Paths. In setting up your marketing strategy, have you brainstormed and researched possible discovery paths, ranging from search to browse, recommend to share, and even interrupt? Which paths are the most important for your company? If so, you are sober. If not, you are drunk - really drunk.

Alternative Consideration. AdWords has a huge marketing budget so it speaks loudly. Yet it may not generate the best ROI. Have you considered all alternatives, ranging from AdWords to SEO, the Display Network to social media? And on media such as YouTube, Facebook, or LinkedIn, have you distinguished between free tactics such as social media marketing and paid tactics such as advertising? If so, you are sober. If not, you are drunk - really drunk.

Measure, measure, measure. We live in an era of measurement, and the great thing about online advertising is the ability to measure. Once you have begun a marketing plan, have you measured it in terms of inbound traffic and conversions? Have you compared one channel to another, not only in terms of traffic or conversions but also in terms of ROI? If so, you are sober. If not, you are tipsy if not drunk.

Considering all alternatives is both the end, and the beginning, of effective online advertising. Take the sobriety test online at http://jm-seo.org/4 or begin your learning journey with our free AdWords MOOC / Tutorial at http://jm-seo.org/67.

AdWords Resources

AdWords, of course, is Google's pay-per-click advertising program. You pay if, and only if, someone clicks on your ad. That's the good news. The bad news is that AdWords can be very complicated and the Google AdWords interface is riddled with "gotchas" and hard-to-find tips and secrets that can make your AdWords campaign incredibly expensive or incredibly effective. Here is our list of the best free resources on AdWords, with the most valuable resources listed first, updated: October, 2013.

If you know of any AdWords resource or tool that we've missed, please email us a suggestion via http://www.jm-seo.org/about/email.html, info@jm-seo.org, or just call 510-713-2150. For more information on the JM Internet Group visit http://www.jm-seo.org/. Thanks!

GOOGLE PARTNERS (ADWORDS PROGRAM)
http://gcptransition.appspot.com/

> Especially if you are involved in AdWords, the new Google partners program is a wonderful resource. Sign up, log in, and gain access to in-depth informative YouTube videos and how to materials on AdWords. Even if you are not an agency, sign up just to gain access to the learning materials!

> **Rating:** 5 Stars | **Category:** resource

SPYFU - http://www.spyfu.com/

> Spyfu will track your ads and competitors ads. Similar to Keyword-spy.com but not as good. Nonetheless, input a competitor's domain and you can see their ads and some basic information on their key-words and bids.

> **Rating:** 5 Stars | **Category:** tool

QUALITY SCORE - WHAT IS IT? THE GOOGLE VIEW
http://bit.ly/MgNauV

The AdWords system calculates a 'Quality Score' for each of your keywords. It looks at a variety of factors to measure how relevant your keyword is to your ad text and to a user's search query. A keyword's Quality Score updates frequently and is closely related to its performance. In general, a high Quality Score means that your keyword will trigger ads in a higher position and at a lower cost-per-click (CPC).

Rating: 5 Stars | **Category:** overview

KEYWORD SPY - http://www.keywordspy.com/

KeywordSpy currently operates in USA, United Kingdom, Australia and Canada. Through this keyword tool and keyword software, you can perform advanced keyword research and keyword tracking to study what your competitors have been advertising in their Adwords campaigns and Other PPC campaigns. You can now get complete in-depth analysis, stats, budget, affiliates & ad copies of your competitors.

Rating: 5 Stars | **Category:** tool

ADWORDS HELP CENTER
http://support.google.com/adwords/?hl=en

This is your gateway to easy-to-use lessons about the Google AdWords advertising program. Whether you're just getting started with AdWords, seeking to improve your ad performance, or studying for the Google Advertising Professionals exam, you'll find lessons designed to help you learn at your own pace. You can also read the complete version (with all available lessons). Just pick a Learning Center version below to get started.

Rating: 5 Stars | **Category:** resource

DYNAMIC KEYWORD INSERTION
http://bit.ly/1aVPQXC

Huh? Dynamic Keyword Insertion can save you time (but cost you money) by replicating the search keyword automagically into your ad. Here is Google's overview of this important, but hard-to-understand, technical feature in AdWords.

Rating: 4 Stars | **Category:** overview

ADWORDS - LEARN WITH GOOGLE
http://www.google.com/ads/learn/

Interested in learning more about AdWords? Similar to Google's IQ
Tests for Analytics, this multimedia site is a fantastic venue of help
articles and video explanations. That's the upside. The downside
is that the site is VERY salesy. So everything is seen through super
positive, Google glasses. It's selling you as much as teaching you
about AdWords.

Rating: 4 Stars | **Category:** resource

ADWORDS CERTIFICATION PROGRAM STUDY GUIDE
http://bit.ly/1d3ZvrV

Boy, that's a mouthful! Google has an offiicial AdWords certifica-
tion program, and for $50 you can take their test and be officially
certified. Even if you don't want to take their test, their official study
guide is a treasure trove of useful information on AdWords. Highly
recommended, and the study guide is FREE. Just remember to put
AdWords in context of other (FREE) efforts like SEO!

Rating: 4 Stars | **Category:** resource

ADWORDS BLOG (GOOGLE OFFICIAL)
http://adwords.blogspot.com/

The official blog for Google AdWords. It's a bit more for sophisticat-
ed users than for newbiews, but - that said - you should pay attention
to it if you are spending money with Google.

Rating: 4 Stars | **Category:** blog

ADWORDS WEBINARS (FREE!) BY GOOGLE
http://bit.ly/KZ8oMj

Like to learn? Keep up-to-date with the latest and greatest in Ad-
Words with this list of upcoming LIVE webinars by Google on
AdWords.

Rating: 4 Stars | **Category:** resource

ADWORDS PREVIEWER - http://adwordspreview.com/

Of course, you can log into your AdWords account and preview ads. But this nifty tool lets you do that without logging in, plus gives you a preview of what the ad will look like on a mobile device. It also warns you on common violations of Google policy like All Caps.

Rating: 4 Stars | **Category:** tool

SEM RUSH - http://www.semrush.com/

Similar to keywordspy, this tool allows you to enter a domain or a competitor, and it gives back a list of AdWords keywords that they are running under as well as their organic keywords. Use it to track a competitor, as well as to generate a keyword list (keyword discovery).

Rating: 4 Stars | **Category:** tool

ADWORDS BROAD MATCH WITH MODIFIER TOOL
http://bit.ly/M1qzlt

Have a long list of keyword / keyword phrases that did not correctly use the + sign? This tool allows you to copy / paste a list of keywords and then it will automatically add the + sign, so 'presto' you can instantly convert to the more focused broad match with modifier.

Rating: 4 Stars | **Category:** tool

ADWORDS EXPERIENCED ADVERTISERS
http://bit.ly/1dH3MRP

Not really sure why it's called 'Experienced.' This is really a collection of informative videos, FAQ's, and free webinars on and about AdWords. All of course with the caveat that it's by Google, so it's somewhat salesy. But still some good information on Google AdWords.

Rating: 3 Stars | **Category:** resource

MICROSOFT AD CENTER / BING - http://bit.ly/MgQdTX

Learn about, and set up, your BING paid advertising.

Rating: 3 Stars | **Category:** resource

WORDSTREAM NEGATIVE KEYWORD TOOL
http://bit.ly/1f4pnWU

Enter your core keyword and this tool gives you 'food for thought' in terms of possible negative keywords. Negative keywords are critical for AdWords, since you pay per click - use this tool to help you find words you DO NOT WANT.

Rating: 3 Stars | **Category:** tool

ADWORDS EDITOR, FROM GOOGLE - http://bit.ly/1jyRnb5

According to Google - AdWords Editor is a free Google application for managing your AdWords campaigns. Use it to download your account, update your campaigns with powerful editing tools, then upload your changes to AdWords. Work offline, then upload your changes any time. Make bulk changes (such as updating bids or adding keywords) in just a few steps. Copy or move items between ad groups and campaigns. Navigate through...

Rating: 3 Stars | **Category:** tool

ADWORDS SEMINARS FOR SUCCESS (AND ANALYTICS)
http://bit.ly/1eXM8NQ

AdWords and Analytics training by Google for Google. A bit salesy (especially the AdWords seminars), but still a useful vehicle to learning more about AdWords and/or Analytics. seminars for AdWords, Google Analytics and Website Optimizer. For details please go to: AdWords 101 & 201: Beginner & Intermediate AdWords 301 &; 302: Advanced Analytics 101: Introduction & User Training Analytics 201: Advanced Analysis...

Rating: 3 Stars | **Category:** resource

ADWORDS ON FACEBOOK - http://www.facebook.com/adwords

Google's official AdWords page on Facebook. If you are into AdWords, then you should 'like' the AdWords page on FB.

Rating: 3 Stars | **Category:** resource

MATCHPEG'S ADWORDS GENERATOR - http://bit.ly/1aVQJPK

Got a list of keywords? Want to create a list of them in phrase match? This nifty tool will do that for you.

Rating: 3 Stars | **Category:** tool

GOOGLE ADWORDS ON TWITTER - https://twitter.com/adwords

Can't get enough official AdWords information? Up late at night? Follow official Google AdWords on Twitter!

Rating: 3 Stars | **Category:** resource

ADWORDS COMMUNITY
https://www.en.adwords-community.com/

This is the official Google AdWords community group, wherein users post questions and get answers from Googlers or other AdWords guru's on AdWords. It's a bit of a free-for-all but useful if you have a burning question about AdWords! Just remember that these are Google forums, so things can be on the salesy side.

Rating: 3 Stars | **Category:** resource

ASK HOWIE - ADWORDS ROI CALCULATOR
http://bit.ly/1eoLAJa

How much should you bid per click? How much do you make per sale? What's your click thru rate? Howie Jacobson is one of the best authors on Google AdWords. This tool helps you figure out your best ROI and bidding strategy.

Rating: 3 Stars | **Category:** tool

DYNAMIC KEYWORD GENERATOR TOOL - http://bit.ly/1cj9Pk4

The Dynamic Keyword Phrase Generator enables you to plug in your primary, secondary and even tertiary keyword phrases. All you need to do is enter in these keyword phrases, separated by comma (,) into the appropriate fields and click generate below. The Dynamic Keyword Phrase Generator will develop a robust list that you can copy and paste into your program of choice.

Rating: 3 Stars | **Category:** tool

GOOGLE ADSENSE SANDBOX - http://ctrlq.org/sandbox/

Looking for ad ideas? This tool allows you to input keywords and see relevant Google AdSense ads. Useful for spuring keyword discovery for SEO (get keyword ideas), as well as helping you to draft effective AdWords ads.

Rating: 2 Stars | **Category:** tool

ADWORDS GRANTS FOR NON-PROFITS (GOOGLE GRANTS)
http://www.google.com/grants/

Google Grants is the nonprofit edition of AdWords, Google's online advertising tool. Google Grants empowers nonprofit organizations, through $10,000 per month in in-kind AdWords advertising, to promote their missions and initiatives on Google.com.

Rating: 2 Stars | **Category:** resource

ADWORDS ENGAGE PROGRAM (OFFICIALLY: GOOGLE ENGAGE) - http://www.google.com/ads/engage/

This program is more for agencies than for businesses. But if you can join it, then you will get access to insider Google information. It's all a sales tool to sell more people on AdWords, but still - there must be some good info in here somewhere, right? After all it's Google's own resource.

Rating: 2 Stars | **Category:** resource

ADWORDS WRAPPER - http://www.adwordswrapper.com/

Use this tool to take your basic keyword list, and then wrap them in the varrious target keyword match types in AdWords (such as quotes or brackets). Unfortunately, does not yet offer the plus for 'broad match with modifier.'

Rating: 1 Stars | **Category:** tool

~ Jason McDonald, Ph.D.

www.ingramcontent.com/pod-product-compliance
Lightning Source LLC
Chambersburg PA
CBHW040815200526
45159CB00024B/2980